This book belongs to

____

For Matt and Oskar

ORCHARD BOOKS

First published in Great Britain
in 2023 by Orchard Books

10 9 8 7 6 5 4 3 2 1

A CIP catalogue record for this book
is available from the British Library.
HB ISBN 978 1 40836 421 5
PB ISBN 978 1 40836 422 2
Published in paperback in 2024

Printed and bound in China

FSC MIX
Paper from responsible sources
FSC® C104740

Orchard Books
An imprint of Hachette Children's Group
Part of Hodder & Stoughton Limited

Carmelite House
50 Victoria Embankment
London EC4Y 0DZ

An Hachette UK Company
www.hachette.co.uk
www.hachettechildrens.co.uk

Waiting for Froggo

Alice Courtley

ORCHARD

Hello, Rabbit! What are you doing?

Oh hi, Mouse. I'm waiting for Froggo.

Oh, how exciting! Can I wait too?

Only if you promise to be very quiet.
I need to concentrate on my waiting.

Okay, Rabbit. I'll be VERY quiet.

1000 PUZZLE

Rabbit, are you sure this is where you're meeting Froggo?

Yes.

Can we play a VERY QUIET game while we wait?

We can't.

Why not?

Because I'm waiting for Froggo.

But, Rabbit. . . what exactly IS a Froggo?

Is Froggo . . . tall? **No.**

Is Froggo . . . hairy? **No.**

Is Froggo . . . smelly? **No.**

Is Froggo . . . invisible? **No.**

Is Froggo . . . famous?

Yes.

REALLY, RABBIT?

No, Mouse.

Look over there, Rabbit!

I can't. I'm too busy.

What do you think they're all doing?

I don't know.

Well, it looks fun. Let's join in!

No. We can't.

Why not?

Because I'm **waiting** for Froggo.

But, Rabbit . . . what if Froggo doesn't come?

But Froggo *has* to come!
Otherwise
all my
waiting
would be . . .

for nothing.

That's not true, Rabbit!
You can do something while you wait.

Maybe you're right, Mouse,
but what would I do—

Mouse?

Yes, Rabbit?

Is that . . .
a bouncy castle?
I *like* bouncy castles.

Hm, this is actually quite fun . . .

Um, Rabbit?

Maybe I should do this again some time!

. . . Rabbit? Look!

Not now, Mouse.
Can’t you see I’m busy
not waiting for Froggo?

But Rabbit, look . . .

UP!

Froggo!

I knew you'd come!

I never doubted it for a second!
What did I tell you, Mouse?
It's actually Froggo!

I've been waiting so long, Froggo,
I just can't wait to hear what
you have to say . . .

Froggo!
Shh!
Listen!

Ribbit.

What do we
do now, Rabbit?

Was that it?!
Yawn!

Hello, what are you all doing?

Us? We're waiting for Doggo.